Spot the Differences
Llama or Alpaca?

by Jamie Rice

Bullfrog Books

Ideas for Parents and Teachers

Bullfrog Books let children practice reading informational text at the earliest reading levels. Repetition, familiar words, and photo labels support early readers.

Before Reading

- Discuss the cover photo. What does it tell them?
- Look at the picture glossary together. Read and discuss the words.

Read the Book

- "Walk" through the book and look at the photos. Let the child ask questions. Point out the photo labels.
- Read the book to the child, or have him or her read independently.

After Reading

- Prompt the child to think more. Ask: What did you know about llamas and alpacas before reading this book? What more would you like to learn?

Bullfrog Books are published by Jump!
5357 Penn Avenue South
Minneapolis, MN 55419
www.jumplibrary.com

Library of Congress Cataloging-in-Publication Data

Names: Rice, Jamie, author.
Title: Llama or alpaca? / by Jamie Rice.
Description: Minneapolis, MN: Jump!, Inc., [2023]
Series: Spot the differences | Includes index.
Audience: Ages 5–8
Identifiers: LCCN 2022011727 (print)
LCCN 2022011728 (ebook)
ISBN 9798885241731 (hardcover)
ISBN 9798885241748 (paperback)
ISBN 9798885241755 (ebook)
Subjects: LCSH: Llamas—Juvenile literature.
Alpaca—Juvenile literature.
Classification: LCC QL737.U54 R535 2023 (print)
LCC QL737.U54 (ebook) | DDC 599.63/67—dc23/eng/20220413
LC record available at https://lccn.loc.gov/2022011727
LC ebook record available at https://lccn.loc.gov/2022011728

Editor: Katie Chanez
Designer: Emma Bersie

Photo Credits: Isselee/Dreamstime, cover (left); Thomas Devenish/Shutterstock, cover (right); a_v_d/Shutterstock, 1 (left); Wasim Muklashy/Shutterstock, 1 (right); Frank Lane Picture Agency/SuperStock, 3, 12–13; La Su/Shutterstock, 4; Rita_Kochmarjova/Shutterstock, 5; colacat/Shutterstock, 6–7 (top), 23br; Harry Zimmerman/Shutterstock, 6–7 (bottom); buteo/Shutterstock, 8–9, 23tr; Sensorman/Shutterstock, 10–11, 23bl; Travelstoxphoto/Getty, 14–15; Pranodh Mongkolthavorn/Dreamstime, 16–17, 23tl; Vaclav Volrab/Shutterstock, 18–19; Eric Isselee/Shutterstock, 20, 24 (left); GlobalP/iStock, 21; Harald Toepfer/Shutterstock, 22 (left); Fotorince/Dreamstime, 22 (right); murbansky/Shutterstock, 24 (right).

Printed in the United States of America at Corporate Graphics in North Mankato, Minnesota.

Table of Contents

Llamas' heads do
not have much hair.

Alpacas' heads
have a lot of hair.

Which are these?

How to Use This Book
In this book, you will see pictures of
both llamas and alpacas. Can you tell
which one is in each picture?

Hint: You can find the answers if
you flip the book upside down!

Many Colors

This is a llama.

This is an alpaca.

Their hair comes in
many colors.

They look alike.

But they have differences.

Can you spot them?

Let's see!

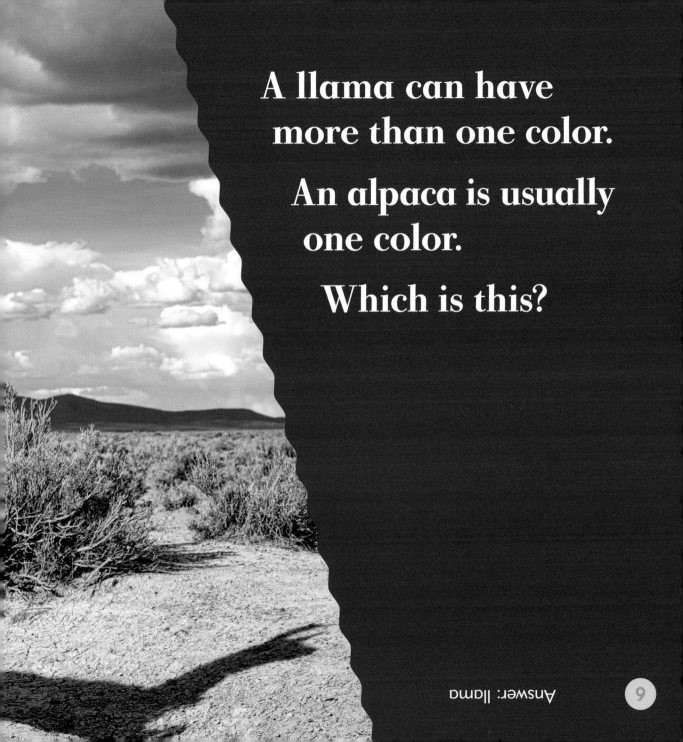

A llama can have more than one color.

An alpaca is usually one color.

Which is this?

A llama's muzzle is long.
An alpaca's is short.
Which is this?

muzzle

Llamas' heads do not have much hair.

Alpacas' heads have a lot of hair.

Which are these?

13

A llama's ears are long and curved.

An alpaca's are short and pointy.

Which is this?

ear

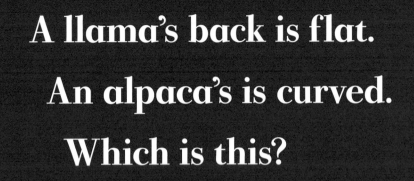

A llama's back is flat.
An alpaca's is curved.
Which is this?

A llama's tail sticks up.
An alpaca's hangs down.
Which is this?

Answer: llama

tail

19

See and Compare

less hair on head

long, curved ears

tail that sticks up

flat back

long muzzle

more hair
on head

short,
pointy ears

curved back

tail that
hangs down

short
muzzle

Quick Facts

Llamas and alpacas are mammals. They both eat plants. They are similar, but they have differences. Take a look!

Llamas

- can be up to six feet (1.8 meters) tall
- can weigh up to 250 pounds (113 kilograms)
- hair can be shades of white, brown, black, or red
- humans use them to carry items

Alpacas

- can be up to five feet (1.5 meters) tall
- can weigh up to 145 pounds (66 kilograms)
- hair can be shades of white, yellow, brown, or black
- humans use their hair to make clothing

Picture Glossary

curved
Bent or rounded.

flat
Without a curve or bend.

muzzle
An animal's nose and mouth.

pointy
Sticking up or out.

Index

To Learn More

Finding more information is as easy as 1, 2, 3.

❶ Go to www.factsurfer.com

❷ Enter "llamaoralpaca?" into the search box.

❸ Choose your book to see a list of websites.